All The Climate Feels

Treesong

Published by Cranncheol Publishing, 2023

Copyright © 2023 Treesong
All rights reserved.
Published by Cranncheol Publishing.
Print ISBN: ISBN: 978-1-7349820-9-1
Ebook ISBN: 978-1-7349820-8-4

Treesong designed the cover art for this book using a climate warming stripe graphic.

This climate warming stripe graphic was created by Professor Ed Hawkins (University of Reading) and used in accordance with the Attribution 4.0 International (CC BY 4.0) license.

For more information on climate warming stripes, please visit showyourstripes.info.

This particular climate warming stripe shows the rise in global average temperature from 1850 to 2021. The fade to black at the end of the climate stripe was added by Treesong to reflect the uncertainty of the future.

This book is dedicated to everyone
who has taken action in support of climate justice
and to the present and future generations
of human and non-human life
who will inherit the world
created by our choices.

Table of Contents

Acknowledgments..1
Preface..3
The Future Refused To Change...5
Hard Change..8
Here..11
Do Pawns Dream Of Pewter Sheep?................................15
A Moment's Peace..17
Look At The Light...22
Post-Apocalyptic...26
Rejoice!..31
Carbon Bombs..36
When I Was Your Age..43
A Hollowness Lurking...50
Insert Anything But Climate Here..................................54
Survive..61
First It Came...68
Your Carbon Footprint..70
Here Comes The Tide..77
Necessity..80
Kobayashi Maru (Climate Edition)................................86
The World Will Remember...91
Heavy Lifting...97
Possible...99
Quis custodiet ipsos custodes?.....................................104
The Weight Of It All...110
Principalities and Powers..117
When I Die..124
One Day..128
#ExxonKnew...133
The Perfect Climate Justice Tweet...............................137
Read More On Ko-fi...141
Connect with the Author...142
More Books By Treesong..143

Acknowledgments

I have many people to thank for their inspiration and support over the course of the twelve years or so that it took me to write the poems contained in this collection.

Carbondale, Illinois is a town of poets. Thank you to the Transpoetic Playground organizers, performers, and audience members for your love of poetry. I performed many of the poems in this collection at Transpoetic open mics over the years. Transpoetic provided an opportunity for local and visiting poets of all styles and experience levels to perform and enjoy some amazing works. Hearing compelling spoken word poetry on a regular basis influenced my style and inspired me to keep writing. Transpoetic is no longer in session, but the powerful play goes on, and Transpoetic has contributed a verse.

Thank you to my past and present supporters on Patreon and Ko-fi. Your contributions over the years have provided me with both the financial incentive and the inspiration to keep writing. I hope that you've enjoyed reading what I've written.

Thank you to all of the climate scientists, climate journalists, and climate communicators who provided the world with the knowledge that inspired these poems.

Thank you to everyone working for climate justice. Your work has informed and inspired these poems. I hope that these poems will inform and inspire people to work for climate justice.

Most of all, thank you to my wife, Grace Darmour-Paul. The remarkable inspiration and support you've provided over the past decade has made my writing career possible. You're the reason I have a loving partner, a beloved child, a stable house to call home, and so many other good things in my life. I am eternally grateful for your presence in my life and this world.

Preface

This book contains twenty-seven poems that speak to various aspects of the climate crisis and climate justice.

Choosing which poems to include in this collection was easy. Almost all of my poetry, fiction, and nonfiction for the past decade or so has dealt primarily or tangentially with the climate crisis and climate justice.

This is partially the result of a conscious choice to break the climate silence and encourage more discourse on climate. It's also a creative and personal obsession. I can't unsee what I've seen, so I may as well write about it.

I hope that my writing inspires people to learn about the climate crisis and take action in support of climate justice. How you act for climate justice is up to you.

My poems tend to run long. Some readers and critics would say that they run too long. I disagree. As long as they're shorter than "The Raven" and "Song of Myself," I don't consider them to be too long. If my readers request more short-form poetry from me, I will happily oblige.

One poem, Here Comes The Tide, began its life as lyrics to a song featured in my novels. For the purposes of this collection, I have decided to declare that this work is also a poem. If the author says it's a poem, it's a poem.

My poems sometimes include pop culture, literary, and personal references. If you don't notice or understand these references, that's okay. The poems should still be enjoyable without the full context for those references.

If you have any questions about this poetry collection or related topics, I'm easy to find in digital reality. I also occasionally make appearances in analog reality.

In the meantime, I hope you enjoy All The Climate Feels. Thank you for reading.

All The Climate Feels - 3

4 - Treesong

The Future Refused To Change

Change.
Change is strange.
Climate change, social change, spare change
do you dare change
the way you think
the way you live
the power you give
to the man in the suit and tie
who tells you what to buy
and when to cry
and how to die?

A little change goes a long way.
Sometimes a dollar or two
can mean the difference between
feasting
on a hot, greasy, saucy
slice of pizza
or gnawing
on the bleached, brittle, broken
bones of hunger.
And sometimes a degree or two
can mean the difference between
the rhythmic turning
from cool rain to Summer swelter
fiery leaves to frozen branches
and the sudden skipping
from cracked dirt to flooded mud
still wind to twisting tornadoes
noon frost to sweaty midnight

convulsing and contorting
and cavorting through the land
and water and air
shredding cities and forests
mountains and valleys
even the oceans
like some dancing diva of death and destruction
until all the world
lies smoldering and simmering
at her shimmering feet.

This is the future
a future already in progress
as we step on the gas
and add fuel to the fire
of a funeral pyre
that's already
licking at our feet.

For year after year
I raised my voice
and took my stand.
For year after year
we studied the climate
with orbiting satellites
and a global network of supercomputers.
For year after year
we drew countless charts and graphs
shouted countless slogans
signed countless petitions
and marched everywhere
from the cobblestone of Main Street

to the marble halls
of every capitol building in the world.

But the future refused to change.
The future refused to change.
The future refused to change.

And the future is now.
The climate is changing
the dancer is dancing
slashing the world
with insatiable wildfires
and torrential downpours
and feverish spasms
from seething summer sweat
to biting winter frost.
And still
our foot is on the gas pedal
and still
the pistons are pumping
and now
the only change
left in our hands
is the power to change
how many people
we run over
while we crash and burn.

So how about it?
Are you ready for change?

Hard Change

The apocalypse will not be televised.
The little glowing rectangles
that frame our world
carry on at length
about the spring storms
tearing cities limb from limb
and the summer sun
scorching endless acres of corn
but they must be careful
oh so careful
not to connect the dots
not to imply for even a moment
that something may be wrong.

Meanwhile
in the world beyond the frames
the temperature's rising
and the oceans
are rising
and the oceans
are soaking up so much
of our car exhaust
and smokestack soot
that they're becoming
too acidic
for life.

At what point
do we start talking about it?
At what point

do we admit we have a problem?
Is it when
entire island nations
are consumed by the rising tide?
Or do we wait
until the streets of London
and Tokyo
and New York City
start slipping beneath the waves?
Or do we wait
until the cities of the world
are choked with millions of refugees
from the drowning coasts
and the barren fields
and the raging walls of flame
sweeping across the land
where desert scrub and mountain wood
once stood?

But the jobs, they say!
Jobs, jobs, jobs!
Coal will bring us jobs!
And oil will bring us jobs!
And natural gas will bring us jobs!
But what good are jobs
when the corn won't grow?
What good are jobs
when our homes are destroyed
by inland hurricanes?
What good are jobs
when the ocean's dead
and the world's on fire

All The Climate Feels - 9

and the oil runs out
and we don't have a Plan B
and we have no one to blame
but ourselves?
Can you eat that coal?
Can you drink that oil?
Do you think those jobs
will even be there anymore
when the shit hits the fan
and the men who own that mine
or that refinery
flee to the Cayman Islands
with all of the profits
from your labor?

We don't need any coal jobs.
We don't need any oil jobs.
We don't need any fracking jobs.
We already have our work cut out for us
the work of admitting that we have a problem
and solving that problem
one person at a time
one politician at a time
one local farm at a time
one solar panel at a time
one city at a time
one state at a time
one nation at a time.
It's time to stop whining for easy jobs
and start working for hard change.

Here

It can't happen here.
Not here
not now
not in this place
this place
where I've spent so many seasons
and found so many reasons
to live.

This land is my body
this clay soil
that feeds the seeds
that grow the kale
that feeds me
rebuilding every cell
with shades of green.
These waters are my blood
these creeks and streams
rain falling from above
aquifers rising from below
quenching my thirst
and flowing through my heart
to become a part of me.

I have walked these hills
these ridges and hills
bottoms and hollows
farmland and wildwood.
I have met these people
these deep-rooted people

children of farmers
who weathered floodwaters
and dry, cracked soil
children of miners
who breathed soot
and battled scabs
children of freedpeople
who endured beatings
and lynchings and shootings
while marching for freedom
children of students
who shut down a university
in the hopes of stopping a war.

After all of this and more
how can it happen here?
How can they come here
to this place
to these people
to drill their deep wells
to fracture the shale
to fill the deep holes
with truck after truck
after truck after truck
of chemical soup?
I know what it looks like.
I've seen it on my screen
the massive wellheads
devouring farmland and wildwood
the thousands of trucks
drinking clean water
and spitting out poison

the twisted bodies of cows
and piles of pills and bills
the invisible methane
choking the air of an entire world
the staccato stuttering
of neighboring fault lines
trembling in response
to explosions deep underground.
I've seen it all happen
but always over there
out there somewhere
not here.
Here
where my food grows
and my water flows
and so many people I know
call home.
Here
where the wind in the trees
awakened me
to the presence
of a living land.
Here
where cancer isn't just a statistic
where it means I have to look into the eyes
of a mother whose child is sick
where it means I have to hold
a small, delicate human being
who doesn't understand the headaches
doesn't understand the nausea
doesn't understand why
someone thought

it was worth the risk
for some quick cash
or political points.

There are so many
other ways to do this
so many other ways
to turn on the lights
to keep hands busy
to put food on the table.
This doesn't need to happen
not anywhere
and certainly not here.
It can't happen here
and it won't happen here
as long as we're here
to stop it.

Do Pawns Dream Of Pewter Sheep?

I once saw a pewter chess board
with lifelike medieval statues
instead of the usual
simplistic symbolic polyhedrons.
I didn't give it much thought at the time
but on reflection
it made me wonder.

Do pawns dream of pewter sheep?
If I cut a pawn, does it bleed?
Is it made of metallic flesh and bone?
Tiny tin sinews
holding together
a crudely sculpted copper skeleton?
Crimson antimony viscera
splattering black and white marble
every time a pawn is slain?

The chessmaster doesn't pause
to consider the dreams of pawns.
The king and queen
lose no sleep
over fallen pieces
lying next to the chess board.

Is it any different
with living, breathing
rulers of nations
and captains of industry?
When a war criminal

paints colorful portraits
of the soldiers he sent
to kill and die
in some distant desert
does he give any thought
to how long they lie awake at night
or what dreams may come
when they sleep?
When an oil baron
sends yet another black snake
over the lands and under the waters
of the indigenous
does he give any thought
to the visions of their medicine people
or the dreams of their children
cut short by poisoned water
and climate catastrophe?

These are the questions
that haunt the pawns.
For the kings and queens
for the chessmasters of the world
they are nothing.
The knight advances.
The pawn is removed.
The game continues.

Do pawns dream of pewter sheep?
The world may never know.

A Moment's Peace

I saw her cross the threshold.
One moment, she was hidden
deep in the womb
sight unseen
waiting to be born.
The next she was here
right here
right in front of me
summoned into this world
by five days of her mother's labor
five delirious days and sleepless nights
of her mother's labor
aided by the songs of her father
aided by the presence
of her grandparents and uncle
aided by the hands and minds
of doula, nurses, and doctor
crossing the threshold
in a wet gush
of blood and fluid
squirming and wailing
her way into the world.

I knew from the beginning
that she would know pain.
I walked with her
to a room down the hall
where they poked and prodded
her tiny form
bending and pricking

her impossibly small wrists and feet
searching for the veins
that would deliver
life-saving antibiotics
while she cried out
in pain and confusion.
I sang to her
but I knew that it wouldn't
make the pain any less.

And I knew from the beginning
that the world she was entering
was under siege.
Beyond the sterile halls
of the hospital
and the gentle walls
of our home
there was another world.
A world where men with blue uniforms
and shiny metal badges
shoot people down in the streets
even children
because of the color
of their skin.
A world where the indigenous
are driven off of their sacred lands
by rubber bullets and pepperspray
sounds cannons and water cannons
broken laws and broken treaties
all in the service
of a hungry black snake.
A world where bathrooms

are used as an excuse
to say that trans people
aren't allowed to exist
and must be erased by laws
and silenced with violence.
A world where women
are still reduced to objects
flesh to be used and abused
workers to be overworked and underpaid
submissive servants and unwilling vessels
for the whims and needs and seeds of man.
A world where we burn so much fuel
that the air's sweltering
even in winter
and the ocean's dying
and sea levels are rising
and the cities are flooding
and the crops are failing
and we'll be damned lucky
if we can make it
through my daughter's lifetime
without crashing and burning.

I knew.
We knew.
We knew what the world was like.
And maybe knowing what we knew
it wasn't fair of us
to bring her into such a world.

But that's not the only world
she will know.

She will know a moment's peace.
She will know the warmth
of being held in the arms
of her mother and father.
She will know quiet walks among the trees
and laughter among friends.
She will know the sound
of our voices raised in song
to entertain and soothe her.
She will know the sight
of our eyes shining
and faces smiling
at the sight of her.
She will laugh at ridiculous things.
She will cry when she falls
and find comfort
in our words and our touch.
She will know
if only for a moment
that this world
can be a place of peace.
And I will do everything in my power
to give her that moment of peace
before the horror of the world
comes for her.

And I will do everything in my power
to give other children
and other parents
and other adults who were once children
that peace too.

20 - Treesong

And every time
the peace is broken
I will cry until my eyes run dry
and scream until my throat is hoarse
and renew my vow
to do something
anything
to mourn the fallen
and resist the violence
and create a world
where everyone knows
at least
a moment's peace.

Look At The Light

Look at the light, they say.
Look at the light
that it brings into the world.
The light, the heat,
the electricity,
the power to alter reality
in accordance with our will.
From early streetlamps
banishing the shadows of night
to speeding trains
soaring jets
ascending shuttles
interconnected computer networks
that weave their way
into every corner of our lives.

Behold, they say!
Behold the power and the glory
of the era of fossil fuels!
Witness the wonders
of an information age
made possible by
coal-fired power
and internal combustion!
Pay homage
to your new gods
with burnt offerings!
Feed the machines
countless tons of coal
countless barrels of oil

countless cubic feet of gas
or you will be forsaken!
Extract it all
or you will lose your jobs
your shelter
your food
your glowing rectangles
that help you
make sense of the world!
Burn it all
or you will lose the light!

And they're not lying.
At least, not entirely.
They've brought us light.
They've brought us heat.
They've brought us power
beyond the imagination
of most of our ancestors.

But that's not all
they've brought us.

They've brought us
smog, soot, smoke
black lung, asthma
poison in our water and blood.
They've brought us
entire mountains
blasted to pieces
in search of coal.
They've brought us

countless barrels of oil
spilled into our rivers
our groundwater
our oceans.
They've brought us
leaking pipelines
and exploding railcars
and even earthquakes
caused by fracking.

And now
they bring us warming.
Every ton of coal
every barrel of oil
every cubic foot of gas
smothers the world
in greenhouse gases
bringing greater and greater heat
melting the ice caps
sinking the coasts
and blasting everything in between
with floods and droughts
wildfires and hurricanes
wars and famines
and every conceivable form
of human misery
that goes along with them.
And the very wonders
of the age of technology
that they claim to champion
will fall like a house of cards
in the winds of climate change

that their fossil fuels
have summoned.

Unless we stop them.

There are other ways
to bring light.
There are other ways
to bring warmth.
There are other ways
to alter reality
in accordance with our will.
The power of sun.
The power of wind.
The power of water.
The power of people
living hand in hand
with each other
and the land.
These are the powers we use
to end the fossil fuel era.
And these are the powers we use
to create our own light
together.

Post-Apocalyptic

I don't have time for
the climate apocalypse
anymore.

I'm not saying that
the climate apocalypse
isn't happening.
It is.
The business as usual
emissions trajectory
is a death sentence
for human civilization.
The ocean will devour
our coastal cities
and spit out
billions of refugees
searching for new homes
in strange lands
plagued by heat stroke and malaria
starved by decades of drought
inundated by sudden bursts of flash flooding
that trigger flashbacks
of the drowned cities
that these people
once called home.

I'm not saying that
it isn't worth my time.
It is.
I repeat

the business as usual
emissions trajectory
is a death sentence
for human civilization.
Not to mention
the consequences for
the rest of life as we know it.
If I can do anything
to delay this fate
even a moment
to lower those emissions
even an ounce
then it's worth a lifetime
of sleepless nights
and bitter fights
against the most powerful
corporations and governments
ever to stalk the Earth.
It's worth every moment I have.
And every moment I spend
on something else
reminds me of the scene
in Schindler's List
where Schindler is counting
how many lives
he could have saved
by selling his car.

How many lives could I save
by selling my car?

I'm not denying
that it's happening.
I'm not denying
the significance.
That's not what I'm saying.

What I'm saying
is that I don't have time anymore
to lose myself
in visions of destruction.
The time has come
to lose myself
in visions of creation.

I see smooth panels of
crystalline silicon and tempered glass
basking in summer sun
standing tall in winter snow
soaking up scattered bits of sunshine
even through the rains
of spring and fall.
I see enormous steel turbines
rising up
over the crashing
black waves and white foam
of the coastal ocean
rising up
over the rustling
green grasses and amber grains
of fields and prairies
rising up
bringing power to the people

with each revolution.
I see a global forest garden
stitched together
from a patchwork of
reclaimed parking lots
and green rooftops
and backyard commons.
I see billions of people
meeting in town halls
and community centers
and abandoned warehouses
and secluded cabins
and geodesic domes
to eat together
and drink together
and dance together
and play together
and plan together
and figure out the details
of living together
in a fossil free world.

I see all of this
and more.
This is the vision
that I set my sights on.
This is the vision
that leads us beyond
the apocalypse of the mind
and into a place
where maybe
just maybe

we can avert
the climate apocalypse
and find ourselves
in a place
that we can all
truly call
home.

Rejoice!

Rejoice!

Rejoice in the power
of the sun.

Delight in the light
of the golden summer sun
shining on row after row
of corn and wheat
tomatoes and cucumbers
fiery red and orange bell peppers
blueberries, blackberries, strawberries
peach and apple trees
and every other fruit and vegetable
under the sun.

Delight in the light
of the golden summer sun
shining on row after row
of deep blue and black
photovoltaic modules
and rooftops adorned with
coils of solar hot water pipes
and fields of smooth, curved mirrors
concentrating sunshine
on pipes filled with steam
or molten salts
to generate and store
heat and light
well into the night.

Delight in the sight
of entire communities
full of brilliant lights
and household appliances
and glowing computer screens
and cars, trucks, and trains
and server farms
and cell phone towers
and hospitals
and factories
and so much more
all powered by the sun.

When the power of the sun
combines with the power of
the wind, the water, the soil
and the ingenuity of the creatures
that they sustain
all things are possible.

We live in a time
when bitter barons
of oil, coal, and gas
loudly proclaim
that we need to extract
and burn
countless tons
and barrels
and cubic feet
of fossil fuels
in order to survive.

They're lying.

Rejoice in the power of the sun
to dispel their lies!
Shine the light of day
on every word
of their misdirection
and outright deception!
The spell they've cast
over our hearts and minds
has no power
in the light of day!
Let the sun shine
and clear the clouds away!

Insatiable blue-blooded oligarchs
are deploying armies
of cold cash and cold steel
against the power of the sun
because they know that
with the simple power
of our words
the simple power
of the light of day
we can burn away
their entire
fossil fuel empire.

Rejoice in the opportunity
to resist them!
Shine the light of day

All The Climate Feels - 33

on their lies!
Sing and dance
in the path of their machines
in the so-called halls of power
in any space that they poison
with their toxic emissions
of lung-killing pollution
soul-killing fear!

Rejoice in the opportunity
to create something better!
Sing and dance
as you plant community gardens
and install solar panels
and solar hot water
and anything else
that harvests the power
of sun, wind, water, and earth
peacefully, cleanly, sustainably
in the service of human need
and in alignment with
the health of the living land!

Theirs is an empire
built on horrors.
Ours is a garden
rooted in joy
even in the face of those horrors
even in the midst of our own mourning
at the sight
of what they've done
to our land.

34 - Treesong

For we have seen the power of the sun
and we have felt the power of the sun
and we must shine like the sun
to dispel the fossil fuel empire
and make our solar visions
a reality.

Rejoice!
Rejoice!
Rejoice!

The sun is rising
and so are we.

Carbon Bombs

Tick tock
goes the clock
on our carbon bomb stock.

What's a carbon bomb
you say?
A carbon bomb
Is a fossil fuel project
that emits so much carbon
into the atmosphere
that it has the potential
to alter the climate
of the entire planet.

Picture
endless acres of boreal forest
vast expanses of evergreens
spruce, fir, larch, pine
wolves, bears, caribou
hawks, owls, songbirds
rivers and wetlands
unbroken forest
looming in cool morning mist
for as far as the eye can see
drawing down carbon
and providing homes
for so many
forms of life
including the indigenous
who have been there

for a hundred generations.
Now picture enormous machines
machines the size of office buildings
tearing through these boreal forests
strip mining every last inch
injecting boiling steam
deep underground
spewing out countless gallons
of toxic sludge
turning that life-sustaining water
into so much oozing filth
that massive man-made lakes
are carved into the earth
time and time again
just to contain it all.
And picture the consequences
of burning every last drop
of that tar sands oil
rising tides flooding the coasts
wildfires devouring remaining forests
flood and drought
drowning and starving the plains
cities choked with climate refugees
thousands of bodies tumbling into the streets
emaciated and homeless
dead and dying
all because of a massive spike in emissions
in a single region.

Can you picture it?
That's just one
of a dozen or more

carbon bombs
in the world today.
And it's already detonating.
And some people
are already
exploring gulf shores
and Arctic ocean floors
looking for more.

The clock's ticking, folks.
The clock's ticking
and the bombs
are already detonating.
It's like something
out of an action movie.
Mission Impossible
on a global scale.
If we don't defuse the bombs
they all blow up
and it's game over, man.
Game over.

So what do we do?

Carbon bomb
is an apt metaphor.
There are a lot of ways
to defuse a carbon bomb
but a lot of debate
over which wires
to cut first.

One of the ways
is to render fossil fuels obsolete.
News flash: they already are!
Digging up flammable shit
and burning it
isn't the only way
to generate energy.
And food doesn't have to travel
thousands of miles
to reach your plate.
So put up a few solar panels
or wind turbines
on your rooftop
or in your community
or buy your energy
from someone who does.
Get your hands in the soil
plant an edible garden
or a food forest
or buy food from a local farmer
or all of the above.
Grow green power
green food
green jobs
in your community
and when anyone
proposes or approves
another fossil fuels project
another carbon bomb
just say no.

Another way
is to raise your voice.
Sign that petition
send that letter
pick up your phone
and make that call
even though your voice
may tremble.
If you're an artist
make your art
translate all of those
cold facts and figures
about the climate
into luscious sensory experiences
that trigger memories
of quiet walks in the woods
the sound of wind in the trees
the sound of children
laughing and crying
whatever glimpses of reality
will inspire others
to action.

Another way
is to take the metaphor literally.
If these really are carbon bombs,
then cut some wires.
Literally.
Turn a few valves
and shut down the flow
of all tar sands oil
from Canada to America

for a day.
Erect a chapel
or a church, or a mosque, or a synagogue
or an ecstatic Pagan temple
in the path of those pipelines
and worship day and night
until the fossil fuel barons
give up their plans
or drag you away
kicking and screaming.
If they've already laid pipe
do some research
cut through some fences
cut through some valves
burn some construction equipment.
Do whatever it takes
to stop the flow of oil and gas
stop the movement of coal
stop the mass combustion
of the fossil fuels
pouring out of these
carbon bombs.

There are so many ways
to defuse a carbon bomb.
The choice is up to you.
But whatever you do
do something.

Tick tock
goes the clock
on our carbon bomb stock.

Let's defuse them all before time runs out.

When I Was Your Age

Dear little human,
when I was your age
we didn't know about global warming.
Some of the scientists knew
of course.
Scientists have known about
what we now call
the greenhouse effect
since the 1820s.
They've known that
we were warming the planet
with our fossil fuel emissions
since 1896.
#ExxonKnew
about global warming
back in the 1970s.
But of course
they didn't talk about it much
back then.

When I was your age
James Hansen
hadn't given his famous speech
warning Congress about
the dangers of global warming.
Michael Mann et al
hadn't published
their hockey stick graph.
Al Gore
hadn't told us all

any inconvenient truths.
Dozens of celebrities
hadn't traveled around the world
through deserts and jungles
mountains and valleys
drought-stricken farmland
and flooded city streets
searching for answers
about global warming
on a Showtime docudrama
called Years of Living Dangerously.

No, when I was your age
the average person on the street
honestly didn't know about
human-caused global warming
or at least didn't know
much about it.

Oh, how times have changed.

We know so much now.
Scientists have traveled the world
exploring every aspect
of climate science
crossing mile after mile
of frozen sea and tundra
to dig up ice cores
trekking through temperate forests
to count tree rings
launching satellites into orbit
to study the land, sea, and sky

spending countless hours
in front of glowing rectangles
analyzing data
and refining models
and communicating results
to their peers
to the media
to the world.

Anyone who's not
covering their eyes and ears
and shouting "LALALA!"
can learn all about
the rising global temperature
the rising of the sea
and the rising consequences
of our emissions.

The information is there now
and everyone with access
to a glowing rectangle
has a front row seat
for the climate apocalypse.

But what are we doing with it?

Dear little human,
when you're my age
what will the world be like?
Will you still eat chocolate
and other foods
from far away

that are threatened
by global warming?
Will you ever drive a car
with an internal combustion engine?
Will someone still be
digging up lumps of coal
and burning them
to power your appliances?
Or will everything run on
the power of sun, wind, and water?
Will you be on the front lines
resisting
the last fossil fuel projects
this world will ever see?

When you're my age
will the streets of Miami
be converted into canals?
Will parts of Miami
be abandoned ruins
looming silhouettes
of burnt-out skyscrapers
lost in shadows
beneath a moonless sky?
Will the soggy streets
be a laboratory
where people explore
ways to transition
an entire city
from life on land
to life in the intertidal?
Will Houston ever recover

from the 500-year-flood
that submerged entire neighborhoods
shut down refineries
shut down ports and channels
released noxious fumes
into low-income neighborhoods
and won't be waiting 500 years
or even 50
to come again?
Will the people
in low-lying coastal regions
of India, Bangladesh, Nepal
and many other nations
drown and sicken and starve
by the millions
until large portions of the land
are eventually abandoned?
Will New York City
and so many other coastal cities
be successful in their efforts
to build enormous sea walls
and eco-berms
and restored wetlands
to hold back sea level rise
or will they too
succumb to the rising tides?

When you're my age
what will you think
of my generation?
The generation
that watched the world burn?

What will you think of me?
Will I still be there
to answer your questions
about the choices I made
and the life I lived?
I tried to step lightly
in this world
but I did drive
a gas-guzzling station wagon
and take a few trips
on a plane
and raise a child
in a nation
with the highest cumulative
greenhouse gas emission
in the entire world.

When you're my age
will you be there at all?
Or will you be
just another name
on another list
a long, long list
of people who succumbed
to hunger, to disease
to heat stroke, to asthma
to mental illness
to war
all because
a few men in suit and ties
felt a need to profit
for a few more quarters

48 - *Treesong*

by adding fuel
to the funeral pyre
consuming the entire planet?

I don't know the answers
to these questions.
But I do know
they might not be good.

Dear little human,
I will do my best
to prepare you.
And I hope and pray
that at the end of the day
even if the world
is burning
you will still be able to find
your moment of peace.

A Hollowness Lurking

There's a red metal bench swing
in the park that I go to.
It's nothing special
just a simple steel frame
and a wide red park bench
dangling from a pair of chains.
But there's a certain comfort to it
in spite of the cold, hard metal.
It looks out on the rest of the park
from a quiet corner
at the top of a small hill
beneath the shade
of a few trees.

I was there one day
not long ago
when it dawned on me
that this was one of those moments
I would always look back on.
It was such a warm, calm day
for the middle of October.
The sun was shining
and the wind was blowing
stirring the leaves on the ground
and the leaves in the trees.
Squirrels were scampering
from tree to tree
and my daughter
eighteen months old
still exploring the world

was wandering around
picking up acorns
and watching the squirrels
and finding her footing
among the gnarled roots
and tufts of tall grass.

The moment felt timeless
like something from a book or movie
that would serve as shorthand
for the finer moments in life.
It felt completely relaxed
effortlessly peaceful
as light as the autumn wind
and as bright as the rising sun.

But then it hit me.

There was an emptiness to it all
a hollowness lurking
somewhere among the rays of sunlight
filtering through the canopy.
I didn't understand it at first.
How could it be here
emptiness in such a full place
heaviness in such a light place
darkness in such a bright place?

And then it hit me.

This is precisely where it belonged.
This is precisely where I should feel it.

This is a moment of peace
the very peace denied to so many
so senselessly.
There are so many people
who should be sitting with me
on this bench
or another bench like it
or a comfy couch
or a rocky ledge
or a stone wall
or wherever else people sit
in their moments
of unbroken peace.
But the peace is broken
the lives are taken
by guns
by bombs
by famine
by bigotry
by zealotry
by wildfires
by raging storms
by rising tides
by the broken human
hearts and minds
desperate enough
to use these weapons
to break the peace.

As I sit on my bench
on a warm day
in the middle of October

there's a part of me
that remains present
basking in filtered sunlight
breathing the autumn air
watching my child
discover an entire world
with new eyes.
But there's a part of me
that feels the absence
of those who didn't make it
a part of me
that feels their absence
just as tangibly
as I feel the presence
of the wind
the sun
the soil
the trees.

There's nothing I can do
to give them back
their golden moment.
But when I left that bench
I carried that feeling
back with me.
Now I find myself
doing what I can
to ensure that
fewer of those moments
will be taken away.

Insert Anything But Climate Here

Insert anything but climate here.

I want to write about
something other than
anthropogenic global warming
and its nigh-inevitable consequences
for human and non-human life.

I want to write about
my morning jog.
It's different every day.
Sometimes it's a breath of fresh air
an ecstatic ritual
invoking the powers
of ancestors and gods
with every rhythmic pump of my legs
every eager gasp of breath
every pounding beat of my heart
set to the tune of
"We Run These Streets" by Stic
blasting in my headphones
as I float down the road
like a kite riding the wind.
Sometimes I can barely breathe
literally and figuratively
as I lurch my way down the road
huddled against the wind and rain
almost doubled over
with bleary eyes
weary legs

lungs on fire
wondering why
I even bother
when it all still seems so hard
even after all of these years.
But some of the best times
are in the spring and fall
when the timing's just right
and I see the sun rising in the east
setting the sky ablaze
in countless nameless shades
of purple, red, orange, yellow
and everything in between
bathing me in their golden glow
and reminding me of my place
in the course of the day
and the turn of the wheel of the year.

I want to write about
my child.
I see her every day
but every time I see her
she keeps changing.
She goes from rolling to crawl
crawling to walking
walking to dancing
and climbing
and kicking a ball
and running around
and practically jumping
but not quite
not yet.

The way that she walks and talks
keeps evolving
from those first faltering steps
and that babyish babble
to her first confident strides
out into the world
beyond my grasp
and her growing vocabulary
in two languages
that's already starting
to exceed my own.
When her eyes light up
and her smile
appears out of nowhere
brightening the whole room
and she says my name
"Papá"
with a smile
everything else falls away
and in that moment
I feel as alive
as she is.

I want to write about
my wife.
Not just about the way
she brought our child into the world
after five excruciating days
of labor.
Not just about the way
that I feel
when I look into her eyes

when I feel her touch on my skin
when I feel her body next to mine
when her very presence
stokes my inner fire
or smooths away my tension
until my muscles relax
my stomach stops churning
and the maelstrom
of thoughts and feelings
thundering through my brain
comes to rest
if only for a while.
Those are all aspects of her
that I cherish
but in the end
they're all about me.
I would rather take a moment
to speak to those parts of her
that are uniquely hers.
To speak of the sound of her voice
raised in song
captivating whatever audience
is fortunate enough to listen.
To speak of the sound of her laughter
and the look in her eyes
a twinkle of joy, mirth, merriment
even mischief
as she plays games with friends
or tells stories about
her day, her life, her world
the people she loves
the dreams she has.

To speak of the beauty of her mind
a mind that has at times
worked against her
as minds sometime do
but that has also
led her to so many moments of brilliance
led her to shine so brightly
that she can learn a subject so well
that she can teach it to so many
thoroughly, effectively, systematically
producing an endless stream
of PowerPoints
and handouts
and projects
and learning games
and tests
and better yet
an endless enthusiasm
for teaching
that only rests
when her body demands it
and springs back to life
as soon as she's had
less sleep than I require
just to stay sane.

I want to write about
all of these things
and more.
But I find myself
staring at a blank page
placing my hand on my hollow chest

pacing the ruins of a shattered mind
a mind flooded with charts and graphs
a mind burning and seething with rage
at the senseless violence of it all
until nothing is left but smoldering ashes
a mind overwhelmed by countless refugees
fleeing the constant barrage
of explosive bits of climate-related content
catastrophic scientific discoveries
and dystopian public policies
that threaten to drive
every last bit of warmth
of empathy
of hope
out of me.

But facing this global challenge
facing it head on
and combing the ruins of my mind
for the scattered remnants of solutions
hasn't ruined me entirely.
Not yet, anyway.
So while I still can
while I still have it in me
every once in a while
I want to write about
anything but climate
if only for a moment.

Insert anything but climate here.
Put the message in a bottle

and watch it get swept away
by the rising tide.

Survive

I'm getting tired
of trying to explain
the importance of
charts and graphs.
I'm getting tired
of trying to convince
burnt-out activists
and overworked, underpaid
disillusioned voters
and non-voters
that they need to care about
a few inches of rising tide
a few forest fires out west
a few drowned bodies
washing up on the shores
of distant lands
that they've never
had the money to visit
and probably never will.
I'm getting tired of waiting
for untold millions
to rise up in the streets
and shut it all down
every coal mine
every oil and gas well
every refinery
every pipeline
every office
of the thinktanks
and corporations

and governments
that made it all happen
or knew all about it
and did nothing
absolutely nothing
or worse
while the world burned.

#ExxonKnew
#UtilitiesKnew
#GovernmentsKnew
#TheyAllKnew

I'm getting tired
of talking about it all
and it all adding up to nothing.
So let's keep this simple.
Let's keep this really simple.

Survive.
That's the executive summary
of what I'm trying to tell you.
It's the action item
that we all need to act on.
Survive.

Because if you can see these words
if you can hear my voice
then you're probably not
sitting in the bowels
of one of those multi-million dollar
rich people bunkers

I keep reading about.
You don't have a seat reserved
in a vast underground complex
housed in the concrete and steel
of a Cold War era missile silo
renovated and restocked with
every modern convenience
complete with indoor pools
vast stores of non-perishable foods
hydroponic gardens
fully-furnished gym and rec rooms
well-stocked medical centers
tastefully decorated cocktail lounges
to mix and mingle
with fellow elite survivors
even a wood-paneled wine cellar
for when you want to
kick back and relax
in your underground den
and celebrate your good fortune
or shed a token tear
for the billions left behind
on the surface.

Are you sitting
in one of those bunkers
right now?
Do you have a ticket to one
stashed in your bugout bag
or back pocket?
No?
Then listen up.

Climate change
isn't some abstract problem
that you can deal with
at your leisure.
It's not about charts and graphs.
It's not about people
in faraway lands
succumbing to
the rising tides
the raging fires
the searing heat
the parching thirst
the hollow hunger
the horrors of war.
Of course
it's about those things too
but even if you don't care about
any of that
consider this.
It's about you.
It's about your survival
and flourishing
in a world under siege
by a catastrophe
of our own creation.
It's about
whether you will lose your job
because the economy collapses.
It's about
whether you will lose your access
to food and water

and medical care
because you ran out of money
or your whole state
went bankrupt
or your region
is beset by
torrential storms
raging wildfires
sweltering heatwaves
and other
not-so-natural disasters
that disrupt the flow
of goods and services
that keep you alive
and relatively happy.
These climate-based disruptions
are already happening
to some people
in some places.
If they haven't happened
to you yet
to your home
to your community
to your nation
then either you've been lucky
or some form of privilege
has given you a free pass
for today.
But free passes
aren't free
and they don't last forever.
If we continue on

our current emissions trajectory
the climate as we know it
will crash
and the economy
will crash
and everything
you know and love
will be thrown into chaos
like so many burnt-out buildings
lost beneath the rising tides.

Survive.
Don't wait
for disaster
to come knocking
at your door.
Think about
survival now
your own survival
your community's survival
our collective survival as a species.
Prepare that bugout bag
and buy that share
in a Survival Condo
if you really want to.
But don't stop there.
Take every action
you can
in the here and now
to reduce our emissions
to reduce everyone's emissions

and increase our chances of survival.

First It Came

First it came for the island nations
washing them into the sea
and I didn't speak out
because I didn't live in an island nation
didn't lose my home to the sea.

Then it came for the developing nations
drowning coastal farmland
scorching once-verdant fields and grazing lands
uprooting hungry, weary bodies
that flooded into cities
already overflowing
with the absence
of employment and housing
and I didn't speak out
because I didn't live in a developing nation
didn't live on the drowning coasts
didn't farm or graze for a living
wasn't dragged out of my home
in the dead of night
by the rising tide
and hung out to dry
like driftwood
bleaching in the sun.

Then it came for the poor
in every city and country
of the world
flooding whole villages and neighborhoods
off the map

turning forests into deserts
breadbaskets into dust bowls
fisheries into algal blooms
stalking among the young and old
striking down millions with
heat stroke, asthma, malaria, hunger
or worse
and I didn't speak out
because I wasn't poor
or a farmer
or a fisher
or elderly
or a child
or otherwise among
the most vulnerable.

Then it came for me
and there was no one left
to speak for me.
And when I looked my killer
in the eye
the face looking back at me
was my own.

Your Carbon Footprint

There are so many ways
to reduce your carbon footprint.
So many ways.

You can replace
your old-school
Thomas Edison era light bulbs
with those weird, new, curly
compact fluorescent bulbs.
Or better yet
you can replace them
with bright, shiny, cool-to-the-touch
light emitting diodes
LEDs
which use a fraction of the electricity
and will probably last
longer than I will.

Or you can become a climavore
which is like a locavore, but better
eating mostly or entirely
foods with a low carbon footprint.
Less meat, less cheese
less baked potato, oddly enough
less of anything
that takes a lot of fuel
to grow, transport, or cook
and more of every green growing thing
grown by your local farmers.
Get to know your local farmers

meet them at the farmers' market
find out what's in season
buy as much as you can
and store the rest of it
in a jar, or freezer, or a root cellar
to get you through
those long, cold winter nights.

Or you can stop driving
that gas-guzzling
carbon dioxide spewing
tailpipe on wheels
you call a vehicle.
You can get an electric car
sleek, smooth, silent
if you have the money for it
or you can ride the bus
if your town has buses
and the routes work for you
or you can walk and bike everywhere
if you're able-bodied
and live in a magical world
where everything you need
is within walking or biking distance
and pedestrians and cyclists
aren't in constant danger
of becoming roadkill.

But all of these options
have their limits.
You see
they're all based

on the same premise.
They all reduce
your personal emissions.
So once you've done it
once you've reached zero
that's it.
Game over.
That's all you can do.

Unless, of course
you go negative.

If you reduce
other people's emissions
enough to offset
your own emissions
and then you keep going
your carbon footprint
will start to go negative.

Sounds great, right?
But how do you do it?

You can take the easy route.
You can buy some carbon offsets.
You'll get a nice, nifty
frameable certificate
talking all about
how many trees you planted
or how many solar panels you installed
or whatnot.
In theory

carbon will be sequestered
and net emissions
will go down.
Your carbon footprint
will go negative.

But does it really work?
Does that little certificate
really mean
less CO_2 in the air
or is it just
a fancy piece of paper
that doesn't really stop anyone
from spewing more greenhouse gases
to cancel out your offsets?

If you have your doubts
you can always try
the direct route
the only sure-fire path
to a negative carbon footprint.

You can go to the source.

You can find someone
who's emitting high volumes
of greenhouse gases
and stop them.
You can sue the fossil fuel companies
for their criminal conspiracy
to deceive the public
and profit from their pollution.

Any judgment against them
will limit the resources
they have available
for more drilling and mining.
Or you can find a pipeline
that's under construction
and chain yourself to the pipes
or the roads
or a dozen of your best friends.
Shutting it down
for even a day
will delay those emissions
and maybe even stop them.
Or you can find a valve
that controls the flow
of massive amounts of oil
and turn that big metal wheel
until the oil stops flowing.
Whether you send out
a press release about it
or sneak off into the woods
before anyone's the wiser
is your call.
Or you can go
on a merry monkeywrenching spree
finding critical
fossil fuel extraction
and transportation sites
slashing tires, drilling holes
cutting wires
burning bulldozers
whatever it takes

to delay or disrupt
the flow of fossil fuels.
Or you can break into
the corporate headquarters
of your favorite oil & gas company
wielding a solar-powered electric chainsaw
running around naked
with wild eyes and a gleeful grin
like Patrick Bateman in American Psycho
letting the blood
of the fleeing corporate officers
flow freely through the halls
like so much oil
spilling in the Gulf of Mexico
or the Arctic Circle
leaving behind
such blood-splattered carnage
that every fossil fuel funder
in the world
will tremble in fear
at the mere thought
of an oil rig or coal mine.
The entire industry
will grind to a halt
and you'll have
the single biggest
negative carbon footprint
in all of human history.

As you can see
there are so many ways
to reduce your carbon footprint.

So many ways.
What's your favorite?
The choice is up to you.

Here Comes The Tide

I walked the streets of New Orleans
The day Katrina came
I knew that the Big Easy just
Would never be the same
The politicians shrugged it off
And said they weren't to blame
The politicians lied
Here comes the tide

Here comes the tide
Here comes the tide
To these sandy, sandy shores
Where so many people died
Each storm is worse
Each car's a hearse
Because the politicians lied
Here comes the tide

The night that Sandy came ashore
I could not comprehend
How these beloved New York streets
Could be the same again.
The corporations told us
Fossil fuels were our friend.
The corporations lied
Here comes the tide.

Here comes the tide
Here comes the tide
To these sandy, sandy shores

Where so many people died
Each storm is worse
Each car's a hearse
Because the corporations lied
Here comes the tide.

Harvey, Irma, and Maria
All came in one year.
The storms were getting so much worse
It seemed the end was near.
The TV called for charity
But told us not to fear.
The media all lied
Here comes the tide.

Here comes the tide
Here comes the tide
To these sandy, sandy shores
Where so many people died
Each storm is worse
Each car's a hearse
Because the media all lied
Here comes the tide.

The world is growing weary
Of this flooding and these storms
We suffer new catastrophes
With each degree it warms
These droughts and fires and plagues and wars
Must not become the norm
The politicians lied
The corporations lied

The media all lied
So let's shut off the pipelines and
Close every last coal mine
New turbines and solar arrays
Will power us just fine.
The wind will blow, the water flow
We'll bask in the sunshine
The politicians lied
The corporations lied
The media all lied
We will not be denied
Here comes the tide

Here comes the tide
Here comes the tide
We will sweep away the oil
And the many men who lied
The oceans rise
Now so will I
Because so many people died
Here comes the tide
Here comes the tide
Here comes the tide

Necessity

Somewhere
in the middle of a field
in rural Minnesota
there is a valve.
A thick metal chain
wraps around the spokes
of the big metal wheel
that controls the valve.
The chain holds the wheel in place
keeping the oil flowing.
The valve is waiting
in silent stillness
in the middle of that field
for days, weeks, months, years
waiting to stop the flow
of that high-pressure
tar sands crude oil
in case of emergency.

Does climate change
count as an emergency?

A handful of people
walk down the long road
that leads to that valve.
Beneath a gray October sky
these Valve Turners hop a metal gate
and walk down the road
to a patch of bare dirt
surrounded by a chain-link fence

topped with barbed wire
adorned with white signs
with bold black and red letters
announcing that this patch of dirt
is owned by an energy company
and the valve contained therein
is only to be used
in case of emergency.

Does climate change
count as an emergency?

When the Valve Turners
reach the chain link fence
they lift their bolt cutters
and cut through a single link
of the metal chain
holding the gate closed.
The chain falls away
and they open the gate
and approach the pipeline valve.
They cut through another link
on another chain
woven through the spokes
of the big metal wheel
that controls the valve.
The chain falls away
and the wheel
is free to turn.
The Valve Turners
turn that wheel
slowly but surely

straining with the effort
of shutting off the flow
of a river of viscous crude oil
flowing through a pipe
under the soil
beneath their feet.

They are not alone.
In other fields
in other states
other Valve Turners
do the same
cutting chains
and scaling fences
to reach the valves
and stem the flow
of that tar sands crude oil
from Canada
to the United States.
Many hands move as one
spinning the wheels
and stopping the flow
of all tar sands crude oil
across the border
if only for a day.

For better or worse
the Valve Turners
turn themselves in.
They hold out their hands
to be cuffed
so that they can be hauled away

and locked in a small room
and paraded before a judge
as alleged criminals.
They surrender themselves freely
in the hope that their actions
in the field and in the courtroom
will help stem the flow
of tar sands crude oil
once and for all.

In that rural Minnesota courtroom
beneath the glare of fluorescents
amidst the hum of central air
powered by the burning of fossil fuels
someone will make the argument
that it wasn't necessary
to walk past those signs
to cut those chains
to turn that valve
to stop that oil.
They will say
that there wasn't an emergency
in the middle of that quiet Minnesota field
that there was no imminent threat
to anyone's health or safety
that the Valve Turners
should have written a letter
or signed a petition
or held up a sign.

But we've written letters.
We've signed petitions.

We've held up signs.
And even after all of that
somewhere
in the middle of a field
in rural Minnesota
and North Dakota
and Montana
and Washington
there are pipelines
where millions of barrels
of tar sands crude oil
are flowing
right beneath our feet
right under our noses
to be burned on our soil
filling our air
with enough CO_2
to heat the entire world
to melt prehistoric ice
to raise sea levels
to drown the coasts
and the people who live there
to bring needless climate chaos
death and destruction
crashing and burning
into the lives
of eight billion people.

The tar sands
are a ticking carbon bomb
and closing those valves
stops that bomb from ticking

84 - Treesong

if only for a day.
If anyone has any suggestions
about how to do that
how to stop that flow
how to stop those emissions
how to stop
those deaths by climate chaos
without cutting those chains
and turning those valves
I'm all ears.

Kobayashi Maru (Climate Edition)

Sometimes
when I think of the climate crisis
I think of the Kobayashi Maru.

Picture yourself
as a starship captain
exploring the final frontier.
You receive a distress signal
from the Kobayashi Maru
a badly damaged vessel
breaking apart
on the edge
of enemy territory.
Do you respond
and risk having
your ship destroyed
in an ambush?
Or do you ignore the call
and risk letting the crew
of the Kobayashi Maru
die before your eyes
when you could have saved them?

In Star Trek
the Kobayashi Maru
is a no-win situation
a grueling simulation
designed to test the character
of a commander under pressure.
No matter what you do

your crew dies in an ambush
or your failure to render aid
leads to mutiny or war.
There's no way to win
only a variety of ways
to put in your best effort
while you go down in flames.

Is climate change like that?

Every day
a billion internal combustion engines
roar to life
in a ceaseless cacophonous chorus
of pumping pistons
and exploding gasoline.
Enormous industrial complexes
burn billions of tons of coal
every year.
It's no wonder
the world is warming
and all it takes
is a degree or two
for millions of people
flesh and bone human beings
to be killed by the warming
drowning in the rising tide
burning alive in wildfires
being blown to bits in resource wars
puking up bile and shitting out blood
because they drank the wrong water
wasting away in refugee camps

littering the streets of strange lands
with their emaciated bodies
and desiccated corpses
because they couldn't find
a bite to eat
or a drop to drink
in a world of plenty.

This is no simulation
no abstract test of character
and the people
who suffer the worst consequences
aren't the ones
sitting in the captain's chair.
We're already in the midst of
this no-win situation
and it seems like nothing we do
is enough
to stop the fossil fuel juggernaut
before it kills
more people than we can count
and sends our entire planet
into a spiral of climate chaos
from which life as we know it
may never recover.

So what do we do?

In the case
of the Kobayashi Maru
James T. Kirk found a simple solution.
Cheat.

Break the rules
Change the parameters
of the system.
Make the no-win situation
winnable.

If the climate crisis
seems like a lost cause
maybe that's because
the people who profit
from fossil fuel extraction
have framed it that way.
Maybe what we need
is a bit of creative reframing
a few daring acts
outside of the box
that transform the situation
into something winnable.
Maybe what we need
is to start from the assumption
that we really will
keep global warming
beneath the daunting
1.5 degree Celsius threshold.
Any system
any economic system
any political system
any way of thinking and living
that's incompatible
with that outcome
needs to be rewritten.

When I look at the latest
charts and graphs
my stomach twists and churns
with anxious rage
not because I think it's impossible
but because I know it's possible
and I have some sense
of what it will take
to get from where we're headed
to where we need to be.

We've got a lot of writing to do.

The World Will Remember

The world will remember
what happened here.

The world will remember
when families came to us
mothers, fathers, children, babies
walking hand in hand
fleeing a land
with too many bullets
and not enough places to hide
the tender flesh, heart, and mind
of a small child.

The world will remember
what was done to them
what was done to those parents
what was done to those children
what was done in our name
what we did or didn't do
to prevent it.

The world will remember
the chain-link fences
with huddled masses of children
wrapped in foil blankets
the rows upon rows of tents
thrown up in border towns
because there were so many children
ripped from the arms
of their parents

the children warehoused
in an abandoned Wal-Mart
with larger-than-life murals
of Donald Trump
talking about losing the battle
but winning the war
and Barack Obama
talking about how America
is a nation of immigrants.

The world will remember
that we told the parents
we were only taking the children away
to bathe them.

The world will remember
that we told the children
they couldn't hug each other
and they had to recite
the Pledge of Allegiance.

I wonder.
Did any of the staff
in the detention centers
see the irony
of forcing a child
living in a cage
to call the United States of America
a nation of liberty and justice for all?

This is not entirely new.
This nation

has been separating
children of color
from their parents
since long before
George Washington
inherited his first slaves.
Every last President
has perpetuated violence
against families of color
in his own way
and every last Congress
and Supreme Court
has done precious little
to stop it.

The details are new.
The big picture
is nothing new.
But that's no excuse
to turn a blind eye
to the latest episode
in a five hundred plus year old
storyline of systemic oppression.

Any time
is a good time
to object
to this white supremacist practice
of separating children of color
from their families.
And any escalation
of this white supremacist practice

of separating children of color
from their families
is a good excuse
to call the whole system
of white supremacist
immigration laws and quotas
into question.

When I see those children
when I hear them crying out
for their mothers
my fists clench
my stomach twists in knots
and my thoughts skip past
the usual calls for vigils and petitions
and fast forward to
visions of occupations
visions of bolt cutters
chain link fences sliced open
under cover of darkness
children and parents
hand in hand
running free
into a world without borders.

And when all is said and done
I also can't help but think about
the day in the not too distant future
when millions of Americans
will themselves be displaced
by rising seas, searing heat
floods, droughts, wildfires, disease

regional conflicts
exploding like firecrackers
among the floodwaters and flames.
It's already starting
and judging by
the rate at which
we keep burning fossil fuels
it'll only get worse.

When we've lost our own homes
when we find ourselves
wandering the world
looking for a moment's peace
a place to rest
our weary heads
will the world remember
this moment?
Will the world remember
that American Presidents
turned away refugees
and refused to acknowledge
our complicity
in the conflicts
that brought these people
to our shores?
Will the world remember
that American Congresses
and American Supreme Courts
all too often
went along with it
or made matters worse?
Will the world remember

that the American people
even on the best of days
could scarcely muster
more than a token amount
of fleeting outrage
a few ignored marches
and forgotten petitions
before moving on
to the next controversy
our glowing rectangles
tell us to debate?

If the world remembers all of this
in our hour of need
I hope they also remember
that some of us did raise our voices.
Some of us did object.
Some of us did march.
Some of us did occupy
the detention centers.
Some of us did organize boycotts
of the people profiting
from the creation and operation
of these camps.

When the time comes
I hope they remember
to show us more compassion
and hospitality
than we showed them.

Heavy Lifting

Thousands of silicon wafers
bask in beams of golden sunshine.
The power of the sun
excites the electrons
in each wafer
and electricity flows
through the contacts.
Mighty motors
spring into action
pulling thick metal cables
attached to
a massive metal cylinder
five hundred tons of iron
dangling in mid-air
in the dank darkness
of an abandoned mine shaft.
When the sun shines
the cylinder rises
storing energy away
for a rainy day.
When the time comes
the cylinder descends.
Electricity flows
through miles of wires
to wherever it's needed.

This is real.
This is a thing that's happening.
Storing and releasing
clean, renewable energy

by lifting and lowering
a massive metal weight.
When I went around
looking for solutions
to the climate crisis
I knew some heavy lifting
would be involved
but this takes the cake.

Possible

It's physically possible.
That's what gets me.
We could all wake up
tomorrow morning
and decide to stop using
fossil fuels.

Of course
there would be
plenty of logistical challenges.
People and products
that need to get places
with electric cars and trucks
and solar-powered airships
that haven't been built yet.
The economy
would be thrown
into chaos
much like the climate
under current emissions trajectories.
Confusion, commotion
riots in the street
people wandering
dazed and confused
among the silent steel frames
clogging the streets
wandering in search of
food and water
and a place to charge
their cell phones

and laptops.

But we could do it.
We could turn it all off
tomorrow
or the next day
or by the end of the year
or the end of the decade.
Every last coal plant
sitting idle
with mountains of coal
left unburned
next to each of them
and endless lines of boxcars
full of jet black rocks
stranded on railroad tracks.
Every pipeline
flowing with thick liquid crude
or natural gas
turned off at critical junctures
by valve turners
unafraid
of turning the wheel
and shutting it all down.
Over a billion
internal combustion engines
sitting idle
in the sprawling parking lots
and long stretches
of blacktop
winding through
every city, county, and province

of the world.

We could shut it all down
tomorrow
and nothing would stop us.
The invisible hand of the market
wouldn't stay our hand
as we turned every valve
flipped every switch
threw the keys
to every car and truck
into the nearest trash can.
No white-robed angels
or silver-suited gray-skinned aliens
or flaming cloven-hooved demons
or other sci-fi or fantasy characters
would descend from the heavens
or rise from the underworld
to stop us.

We could do it.
It's physically possible.
No cosmics forces
would conspire to stop us.
But we don't do it.
We wake up every morning
and flip the switch
turn the key
tap into the power grid
or oil supply
that powers
our miraculous devices

and at the same time
tears our world apart
at the seams.
We do it
because anything else
seems impossible.

But is it really?

Individual and collective choices
are governed
by their own rules too.
But those rules
seem more malleable
than the cold, harsh
immutable laws of physics.
Maybe the odds are against us
maybe it's too late
to make a meaningful difference
in the course of human events
that is currently determining
the course of climate change
for millennia to come.
But the only way
to know for sure
is to try it.

It's still physically possible
to avert the worst consequences
of human-caused climate change.
Let's see what we can do.
Let's build those solar panels.

Let's build those wind turbines.
Let's build that geothermal.
Let's see how far
we can go.
Maybe the softer laws
governing human behavior
will place softer limits
on how much we can change
and how quickly we can do it.
So let's come together
to shift public policy
to shift patterns of consumption
to mobilize millions of people
in the service of climate solutions
and climate justice.
Let's do what we can
and discover together
what's possible.

Quis custodiet ipsos custodes?

Quis custodiet ipsos custodes?
Who watches the watchers?

Satellites
loom high overhead
higher than the mountains
higher than the clouds
higher than even
the other satellites.
They float motionless
in the void of space
quietly watching
listening
whispering secrets
to the watchers
stationed below.

The watchers
lurk behind closed doors
collecting every bit of data
they can possibly find
endlessly crunching numbers
scrutinizing scenarios
formulating elaborate strategies
to achieve their ends
by any means necessary.

But they don't just watch
do they?

They call themselves
the intelligence community
because they want us to focus
on intelligence.
Their intelligence.
The many ways
that they watch and scheme.
The clever ways
that they shift the course
of entire societies
from the comfort
of an air-conditioned office.

I must admit
I find myself in awe
of their ability
to alter the course
of human history.

Calling it intelligence
makes it sound civilized
smooth and sanitary
cool, calm, collected
almost boring, really.
So much so
that we can develop
a vast network
of agencies
buildings
satellites
supercomputers
intelligence personnel

a network with tendrils
extending through the nation
and the world
without most people
outside of that network
giving it a second thought.

But it's not just about
intelligence
is it?

The whole point
of their so-called intelligence
is action.
Covert action.
Surgical strikes
with aerial drones
or special forces
or press releases
blasted out
to alleged journalists
who do little more
than sit around
reading those press releases
and calling it news.
Mass killings
either by our own hand
or the hand of those
we've funded, trained
sold weapons to
knowing full well
where those weapons

would be pointed
and who would die.
Entire nations burn
in response
to acts of aggression
by the intelligence community
and its proxies.
The watchers
say it's all
in our best interest.
National interest.
National security.
But they also say
it's all top secret
and it's not our place
to ask too many questions
or point out gaping holes
in the information
they do tell us.
And their definition
of national interest
seems to be
ever so cleverly aligned
with the interests
of the oligarchs
who fund the campaigns
of the politicians
who supposedly oversee
this so-called
Intelligence community.

Think of what we could accomplish
If we used all of those satellites
all of that infrastructure
all of that people power
to pursue peace and justice.
We could solve the climate crisis
in a heartbeat.
We could find food for the hungry
shelter for the homeless
care for the sick
real rights
for people of all
genders, colors, and orientations
a rapid transition
to clean, abundant energy
for one and all.
We could develop
plans within plans
to ensure
all of this
and more.
Instead
we use
this vast network
of brilliant brains
and miraculous machines
the same way we've used
every new tool
since the discovery of fire.
Burn your neighbor
and take their stuff
before they can do the same to you.

Quis custodiet ipsos custodes?
Who watches the watchers?

I do.
I'm watching.
Other advocates
of peace and justice
are watching.
The whole world is watching.
And if your clever plans
can't withstand scrutiny
in the light of day
then they deserve to fail.

The Weight Of It All

He was quick to smile
at least in the early days
and his smile was contagious.
His eyes were brilliant
shining with a raw intelligence
that was evident
in his every glimmer and glare
matched by the
smooth, silky cadence
of a commanding voice
that will be remembered
for generations.
On another man
those long, lean limbs
might have been awkward
lanky
but he carried them
with elegance.
Every time
he strode up to that podium
the world listened.
Regardless
of how they felt about him
they listened.

We all know
the public persona.
But I find myself
wondering about the man
the flesh and bone human

and how he felt
in his darkest hours
or at least the hours
that I consider
his darkest.

Did that eloquence and confidence
always come easily to him?
Or did he sometimes feel
the weight of his actions?

Did he walk into every meeting
with his head held high
eyes unwavering
voice steady and sure
as he spoke with advisors
about the details of
escalating drone strikes
orchestrating regime change campaigns
backing "all of the above" energy policy
in the midst of a climate crisis?

Or did he hesitate?
Did he waver?
Did he weigh the costs
of signing off on
an extrajudicial hit list
engaging in mass killings
mass extraction and combustion
of fossil fuels
against the cost
of doing nothing?

Did the choice
to drop those bombs
to drill and frack and burn
weigh heavily
on his broad, proud shoulders?

I have images of him
that cameras never captured
but firsthand reports imply.
When he sat down
in the White House Situation Room
on Terror Tuesdays
and studied
drone target data sheets
like so many baseball cards
and picked up the pen
to sign the death warrants
for targets intentional and collateral
did he pause before signing?
Did his steel pen tip
hover for a few seconds
above the paper
making tiny circles in the air
awaiting final orders
as he performed
the final moral calculus
that dropped bombs
on weddings and funerals
deployed special forces
to destabilize governments
altered the course
of entire nations?

Did he ever seek
comfort and confirmation
in the dog-eared pages
of a Reinhold Niebuhr text
about the righteousness
of World War II
while studiously avoiding
any of Niebuhr's passages
critical of the Vietnam War
critical of unilateral action
critical of American exceptionalism
critical of the moral fallibility
of all leaders
and all nations?
Did he ever
lie awake in the White House
haunted by the pictures
before and after
of the targets of his orders
human bodies in other nations
torn limb from limb
by the stroke of a pen?
Did he ever
look at his wife
and his children
and imagine the grief
of those shattered families
shattered nations
and sigh a heavy sigh
and get a distant look in his eye
as some quiet corner of his mind
lamented

the terrible choices
the terrible weight of it all?

As I lie awake
in my own bed
feeling the weight
of those choices
and my role in them
as a citizen of this nation
I wonder if any of the dead
would give a damn
how he felt
when he signed their lives away
or how I felt
while I watched him do it
and did precious little
to stop him.

More importantly
I wonder
how many of the dead and dying
feel the full weight of his actions
in a way he never will.
How many people
spent how many minutes
hours, days, years
feeling the weight
of the looming buzz
of drones flying overhead
the one-ton Predator
the five-ton Reaper
the hundred-pound Hellfire missiles

the skies always heavy
with cold steel birds
ready to strike
the weight of sudden explosions
tearing through flesh, brick, stone.

As I lie awake
I see a family
driving to a wedding.
Dozens of people
pile into cars and trucks
talking, laughing
arms around each other
celebrating love
celebrating life.
In an instant
the full weight
of American presence
in their nation
explodes through the caravan
shredding solid steel
shredding tender human flesh
crushing whole families
in the blink of an eye.

The weight of that
Ivy League moral calculus
is so much heavier
when you're on
the receiving end of it.

In the aftermath
of the explosion
the air is thick
with black smoke
searing flames
the mournful wails
of the living
and the dying
intermingled
indistinguishable.
But somehow
all I can hear
is a solitary whisper
floating on the wind.

"I only felt the weight of it
for a moment, mother.
Now I feel weightless."

Principalities and Powers

I have seen it.
I have seen the thing
that stalks this land
filling the air
with foul fumes
filling the lungs of children
with abrasive particulate filth
choking children and adults
until they can't breathe
altering the climate
of an entire planet
flooding fields one day
and scorching them the next
tearing through cities and towns
with hurricane winds and rising tides
tearing apart the fabric
of human civilization
driving the biggest mass extinction
in millions of years.

If we keep going
on our current emissions trajectory
it may be the biggest extinction ever.

I've seen it.
I've seen this creature
this mad, ravenous, tempestuous creature
stalking our land.
It devours whole forests
for wood to burn

or simply to get those trees
and their neighbors
communities of plant, animal, and fungi
out of the way
for more extraction.
It blasts deep holes into the earth
blast the tops off of entire mountains
to rip up the coal buried within.
It fractures the shale
with underground explosions
pumps millions of gallons of clean water
into each well
thousands of times
for thousands of wells
and spits out wastewater
full of radioactive toxins
so that it can suck the earth dry
of every last bit
of natural gas and oil.
It burns fossil fuels
spews poison into clean water
belches out endless amounts of
smothering greenhouse gases
all in the name of
feeding its insatiable hunger
for energy
for profit
for infinite growth
on a finite planet.

I have seen this creature
and I have come here today

to show you its face.

Some people don't see it at all.
They witness its tentacles
thrashing through the land
and they tell themselves
soothing little lies.
It's not really happening.
It must be a natural cycle.
It's not a big deal.
There's nothing we can do.

Some people do see it
but don't grasp it
not fully.
They want to fight the creature
stalking our land
but they only grasp
a single slippery tentacle.
They say that we must
change a few light bulbs.
Recycle more.
Consume less.
And yes
they have grasped
a part of the beast
and yes
they have found a place
to take action
a way
to drain the creature
of some of its power.

But it's not enough.
They have not seen its face.
I have seen its face.

This all-consuming beast
this devourer of fossil fuels
this spewer of greenhouse gases
this disrupter of global climate
this destroyer of communities
human and non-human
is a creature
that lurks in the realm of
principalities and powers.
Like some eldritch horror
its flesh is made of star stuff
arcane words on parchment paper
giving it form
incorporating it
into a myriad
of ever-changing corporate bodies
each of which is populated
by a myriad
of ever-changing human drones
serving the will
of the creature's corporations.
These drones are not mindless.
They are human beings
fully culpable
for their every word
every action
every form of participation

in the machinations
of these corporations
that form the formless body
of this creature.
But stopping
the individual humans
who serve the corporations
is not enough
to stop the beast.
Take away
a few individual human servants
through legal action
or public pressure
and the creature endures.
There is only one way
to defeat this creature
one sure way
to stop this beast
from devouring
and burning
every last ounce
of fossil fuels
thus rendering
our world
uninhabitable.

Unmake it.

Unmake the beast.
Unmake this creature
in the realm
of principalities and powers.

Track down
every last corporation
whose mission contains
the slightest involvement
in the fossil fuel industry
and revoke their corporate charters.
Seize their assets
as the ill-gotten gains
of a criminal enterprise.
Use the proceeds
to fund a just transition
to clean energy.
And moving forward
let every corporate body
every business
every non-profit
every local government
every state government
every national government
recreate itself
with the principles
of environmental justice
and climate justice
embedded in its mission
and structure
so that the beast
that nearly devoured our world
is forever banished
unable to take form
in the presence
of our active commitment
to live in accordance

with those principles.

This creature I speak of
is a creature
of principalities and powers.
As such
it may at times seem
untouchable, invincible, immortal
to creatures of flesh and blood
like you and I.
But it is none of these things.
It was wrought by human hands
and it can be destroyed
by human hands.
It can be.
It must be.
It will be.
And we are the ones
who will destroy it.
And in its absence
the world will flourish.

When I Die

When I die
don't bury me
in a graveyard.
Don't stick my body
in a cheap pine box
beneath six feet of dirt
beneath a green grass lawn
that must be mown and mown
until the end of days.
I've had my fill
of lawnmowers.

Don't cremate me
and store me ashes
in a fancy metal urn
or scatter them
in the places
that made my heart
go pitter patter
while I still drew breath.
It's a lovely idea
better than most
but the carbon emissions
are more than I care for.

If you must be rid of my bones
in some nearly conventional way
I suppose I would enjoy
a green burial
direct in the soil

124 - Treesong

or a simple hemp sack
with a mighty oak
growing above me
and perhaps one day
wrapping its roots around me.

But really
truly
what I want you to do
with my cold, stiff corpse
is tidy it up a bit
make it look presentable
without embalming
and take it to the nearest
major fossil fuel site
and shove it inside
to gum up the works.

If someone's building a pipeline
or fracking for oil and gas
or building an export terminal
or anything else
that helps the extractive economy
burn more fossil fuels
by all means, take me there!
Dress me up
in a neon green vest
with a hard hat
on my head
and big steel toe boots
on my feet
and a clipboard

full of cryptic nonsense
in my hands.
Toss me
in one of those big steel pipes
or under a backhoe
or in a shallow grave
where they're about to dig.
Hell
shove me
in a Porta-Potty for all I care!
I won't mind the smell.
Make it look like an accident
if you can.
Throw in some props
like a few gallons of blood
like old steel barrels
with radioactive symbols
and a few bucketfuls
of corn syrup
with green food coloring
to fill the scene
with puke green slime.
Whatever it takes
for them to stop production
for a day or two
or half a dozen
while they figure out
what the hell
actually happened.

I don't know where I'll go
when I die

but wherever I am
if you do that with my body
I'll sure be laughing
and if it stops
a bit of the burning
for even a day
the world will be
a better place for it.

One Day

I wake up coughing.

Even after the cough subsides
the acrid smell of smoke
burns my mouth, nose, throat.

I look up
at a sky filled with
churning mountains of black smoke.
I stand up
and look around.

I see blue skies
on the horizon behind me.
The sky above
and horizon before me
are jet black
with smoke so thick and wide
it looks like a storm front
moving in.

I'm standing in a field
up to my knees
in grass and wildflowers.
When I look forward
I see an asphalt road
stretching off into the distance.
There's a white metal road sign
at the start of the road.
The sign has five words

in bold black letters.

"ONE DAY: Start of Emissions"

I start walking down the road.

On either side of me
I see a long row of houses
stretching off into the distance.
The size and style
of the houses vary
but they all have one thing in common.
Each house has
an Olympic-size swimming pool
in the front yard.

The swimming pools
are full of oil.

The oil is on fire.

I walk down the middle of the road
keeping as much distance as I can
between myself
and the thick columns of smoke
pouring into the sky
from the writhing infernos
scorching the land and air
for as far as the eye can see.

I keep walking
expecting it to end.

A few steps
a few yards
a few miles.
More houses
more swimming pools
full of burning oil.

I see families
gathered for cookouts
wearing star-spangled shirts and khakis
cooking burgers on grills
roasting marshmallows
over the open flames.
I see people in ragged clothes
wandering from pool to pool
warming their hands by the fire.
I see men in business suits
drinking champagne
as workers in denim overalls
roll wheelbarrows full of cash
into the men's houses.
I see police in riot gear
chasing people with signs and banners
away from the pools
blasting people with water cannons
and chirping sound cannons
until they retreat down side streets.

I keep walking.

I walk through the hunger.
I walk through the thirst.

I walk until my knees buckle
and then I crawl
across the hot asphalt
until my hands are red and black
with blisters and tar.

With one hundred miles behind me
one hundred miles
of Olympic swimming pools
filled with burning oil
I finally see it.

There's a white metal road sign
at the end of the road.
The sign has five words
in bold black letters.

"ONE DAY: End of Emissions"

This is it, then.
I've walked through
one day's worth of
global oil consumption.
One hundred million barrels.

As I collapse
at the base of the sign
a single thought consumes my mind.

If this is how much oil
the world consumes
how much longer

can it go on?
And when will it end?

One day.
One day.
One day.

#ExxonKnew

The scientist
stands on the deck of
Exxon's largest supertanker
the Esso Atlantic.
After a long day
in the laboratory
he steps outside
for a breath of fresh air.
He looks out at
the churning seawater
stretching to the horizon.
He feels the wind
cooling his face and hands.
He smells the salty air
dispelling the acrid diesel fumes
of the tanker's interior.
He knows
he can't see or feel or smell
the carbon dioxide
soaking into the waters below
but tells himself
that his instruments
will find it.
He will soon know
just how much CO_2
the ocean is absorbing.

After his voyage at sea
the scientist
stands in a boardroom

on dry land
staring at the blank faces
of the men in suits
across the table.
His charts and graphs
words spoken and unspoken
outline the contours
of the near future
a world in chaos
oceans rising
to devour coastal cities
corn and wheat
dying of thirst
in the summer heat
millions of voices
clamoring for an end
to the extraction and combustion
of fossil fuels.
A few of the men at the table
scribble a few notes
ask a few questions
stare off into the distance
with a thoughtful look
in their eyes.
The rest glance at their watches
waiting for the meeting to end.
When it does
the scientist wonders
if anyone actually listened.

He wonders
for days, weeks, months.

He keeps wondering
until he hears the news.

The scientist
fills the cardboard box
with the personal effects
from his desk.
A framed photograph of his family.
A small potted cactus.
A dog-eared green folder
containing a handwritten report
from his daughter's
science fair project.
As he follows
the security guard
into the lobby
it occurs to him
that at least some of
the men in suits
did listen.
He just didn't anticipate
their response
as well as he anticipated
the rise in global temperature.

A quarter of a century later
the scientist sees two words
on his computer screen.
Two words
smashed together
with a hashtag.
#ExxonKnew.

Before he reads the article
the scientist knows
what it will say.
And again
twenty-five years later
he wonders
if anyone is listening.

The Perfect Climate Justice Tweet

I keep searching
for the perfect
climate justice tweet.

For better or worse
so many people
turn to Twitter
for infotainment
packed into
280-character
soundbites.

Sometimes
all it takes to go viral
and be seen and heard
by thousands of people
or even millions
is to say the right words
at the right time.

Secret algorithms
written by Silicon Valley tech bros
employed by billionaires
weigh the value of our words
like Anubis weighing hearts
on the Scale of Justice
minus the justice.

The scales are tipped
in favor of the billionaires

who own them.
But sometimes
all it takes
to speak truth to power
the power of the people
is to find the right words
that tickle the algorithms
while also stoking the fires
of revolution.

So in spite of myself
I find myself
racking my brain
for the perfect climate justice tweet.

280 characters
to make climate justice
the top trending topic
of the day.
280 characters
to inspire the people
to rise up
and tear down
fossil fuel empires.
280 characters
to convict climate criminals
seize fossil fuel assets
bring climate reparations
and just transition
to the people.

So far
I haven't found it yet.
But maybe
if I spend another
280 minutes
doomscrolling
it'll come to me.

Read More On Ko-fi

Thank you for reading All The Climate Feels!

My name is Treesong. I wrote these climate poems. If you liked them, I have good news. I also write climate fiction!

You can read all of my poetry and fiction online at Treesong's Ko-fi. I have novels, short stories, anthologies, poems, and interactive fiction gamebooks available for sale. You can either buy individual ebooks or become a member and read all of my stories and poems for as little as $1 per month.

If you're already a Treesong's Ko-fi member, thank you for your support! Members like you help provide the financial support and inspiration that keep me writing and publishing.

If you're not a member yet, please check out Treesong's Ko-fi today. Members get new content each month plus access to a growing archive of novels, short stories, anthologies, poems, interactive fiction game books, and beyond.

For more information, visit ko-fi.com/treesong.

If you like All The Climate Feels, be sure to check out my other books and connect with me on social media and beyond. In the meantime, thank you for reading!

Connect with the Author

My name is Treesong. I'm a father, husband, author, talk radio host, and Real-Life Superhero. I live in Carbondale, Southern Illinois. I write novels, short stories, nonfiction, and poetry, mostly about the climate.

Thank you for reading my book! I invite you to learn more about my other books and Real-Life Superhero adventures by connecting with me online.

Website/Blog
treesong.org

Social Media
Ko-fi: ko-fi.com/treesong
Facebook: @TreesongRLSH
Twitter: @Treesong
Instagram: @TreesongRLSH
TikTok: @treesongrlsh

Treesong's Newsletter
Get a free short story, sneak peeks at upcoming releases, and other bonus content by subscribing to my author newsletter. It's completely free and takes less than a minute. You'll receive my newsletter via email about once or twice per month along with other perks of being a part of my reader community. Sign up today at treesong.org/subscribe!

More Books By Treesong

Change

What does global warming look like in a world full of magic, superheroes, and secret societies?

Sarah Athraigh, a climate activist from Southern Illinois, stumbles into a war between occult factions that are grappling with the root causes and dire consequences of climate change. She goes on the run and finds herself on a journey of discovery, searching for the unusual allies and innovative ideas that will help her to make a difference for the better in a dangerous world.

Change is a contemporary fantasy tale featuring a strong female lead, real-life superheroes, secret societies, modern magic, political protests, the power of music, and a colorful cast of characters that Sarah meets along the way as she searches for solutions to the climate crisis.

Order

If you had all the power in the world, would you stop climate change?

Truman Stuart is a man on a mission. As the new Preceptor of Order, it's his job to oversee the survival and progress of human civilization. When he discovers that climate change poses an existential threat to humanity, the Preceptor knows that he has to find a way to stop it. But how can he solve a global crisis that his own organization and its powerful fossil fuel allies helped create?

Order is a contemporary fantasy tale featuring a powerful secret society, glimpses of magic and hypertech, an underground resistance called Anomalous Revolution, and a colorful cast of characters that the Preceptor meets along the way as he searches for solutions to the climate crisis.

Goodbye Miami

What happens when the climate crisis turns Americans into refugees?

Kass flees Miami in the wake of a hurricane that leaves the city underwater. After moving in with her cousin in Southern Illinois, Kass struggles to deal with her displacement. She hopes to return to the city that she loves. But thanks to climate change, that city is underwater. What starts as a search for survival soon evolves into a struggle for the future of Miami—and the world.

Goodbye Miami is a political thriller featuring a strong female lead, climate refugees, political protests, community organizing, and creative solutions to the challenges of grassroots climate adaptation in a major city that has succumbed to catastrophic flooding.

Cli-Fi Plus

Cli-Fi Plus is a climate fiction anthology with an emphasis on genre and theme crossovers. Each short story combines cli-fi themes with other elements of sci-fi and literary fiction. The resulting stories keep you on the edge of your seat and leave you wondering what will come next in the real-life climate crisis.

What does a cli-fi alien story look like? What does a cli-fi robot story look like? What does a cli-fi zombie story look like? What does a cli-fi time travel story look like? What does a cli-fi political thriller look like? What does literary cli-fi look like? Find the answers to these questions and more in Cli-Fi Plus!

LEARN MORE ABOUT
TREESONG'S FICTION, POETRY,
AND REAL-LIFE SUPERHERO ADVENTURES
AT TREESONG.ORG

www.ingramcontent.com/pod-product-compliance
Lightning Source LLC
LaVergne TN
LVHW041626070426
835507LV00008B/472